A WONDERFUL JOURNEY INTO CHRISTMAS

25 DAY DEVOTIONAL

LEAH LEVINE

© 2024 by Leah Levine

Cover photo compilation using photos by krcil, Liudmila Fadzeyeva, LiliGraphi/Shutterstock

Cover and interior design by Linda Bourdeaux/thedesigndesk.com

All rights reserved. No portion of this book may be reproduced, stored in a retrieval system, or transmitted in any form or by any means—electronic, mechanical, photocopy, recording, scanning, or any other—except for brief quotations in critical reviews or articles, without the prior written permission of the publisher.

No patent liability is assumed with respect to the use of the information contained herein.

Scripture taken from the New King James Version®. Copyright © 1982 by Thomas Nelson. Used by permission. All rights reserved.

ISBN: 979-8-3454-4344-6

DEDICATION

This book is dedicated to my wonderful family who encouraged me to write this book and to all the wonderful teens and staff at My Friend's House. Thank you for allowing me to come and sit with you while you share your heart. My life is forever changed and I hope you know God loves you and is with you wherever you go.

Proceeds from this book will go to Woven Tree, a non-profit whose mission is to bring life and refreshing to local foster care children, the homes they live in, and the teams that care for them.

SPECIAL THANKS

To my beautiful family, Andy, Samuel, Moses, and Jan, who supported me in writing this book. I pray even when I am gone from this earth that you always know how much I love you, I am so proud of you, and how much I love Jesus.

A PERSONAL NOTE

Christmas time means so many different things to each person. For some, it's a joyful time, while for others, it can be a sad or challenging season. I was never excited for Christmas. For me, it was a cold time of the year and a reminder of the tough things my family had gone through. So, for many years Christmas was beautiful but difficult.

A few years ago, God healed my heart and Christmas came alive to me. His story became my special story. His presence became more real than the gifts, the festivities, and the hype. The season became a beautiful gift to me from Him. No matter how you see and feel about the Christmas season, I encourage you to let it all go and embrace this season in a new way. Let go of all the stress and business. Take a few moments to be quiet each morning and allow each page to speak to you.

This book has 25 readings which allow you to start on December 1st and end on Christmas Day. As you open the pages of this book each day, I encourage you to ask God to speak His heart to you. He hears you, loves you, and wants to meet you this Christmas season. Let go of all your ideas of Christmas and allow Him to show you His heart and reason for Christmas. My prayer is that you see not only the beautiful story but also the great price He paid so that you can know His love for you. Bless you as you learn to enjoy this Christmas season.

Leah

DECEMBER 1

God's Greatest Gift

For unto us a Child is born, Unto us a Son is given; And the government will be upon His shoulder. And His name will be called Wonderful, Counselor, Mighty God, Everlasting Father, Prince of Peace.
—ISAIAH 9:6

God loved the world so much that he gave his one and only Son so that whoever believes in him may not be lost, but have eternal life.
—JOHN 3:16

But God, being rich in mercy, because of the great love with which he loved us, even when we were dead in our trespasses, made us alive together with Christ— by grace you have been saved.
—EPHESIANS 2:4-5

God's heart of love is always reaching out to mankind. As many would say, if God loves us, why does God allow evil to take place, and why do bad things happen to good people? To understand the answer to this question, we must know that God does not force people into a relationship with Him. He doesn't force us to love Him or choose His ways. He is a gentleman and we have free will. In any relationship, we shouldn't force someone to love us or stay with us. Our desire should be for genuine love from someone who truly cares.

The same is true with God. He welcomes and invites us into His story of covenant love and redemption, but it is only an invitation He offers us—not a forcible demand. Because we have a choice, many have turned down His invitation, and the consequence of a world that turns away from a loving God is a world where hate, hurt, fear, and evil can prevail.

For this first day of the Christmas season, may you truly see His loving invitation to you to enter the greatest love story you will ever know. The true meaning of Christmas is not Santa Claus, nor elves, nor getting great gifts, even though all those make the season fun and festive. The Christmas season is an opportunity for us to pause and take a moment to see the real story of God's immense love for us. He showed us this love through His greatest gift to us—His son, Jesus—sending Him to earth to redeem us. Jesus then showed His love for us, by humbling himself to enter the world as a baby, living as a mortal man, and paying the ultimate sacrifice for our sins. Oh, what an amazingly beautiful love story that Christmas is.

As you prepare for all the hustle and bustle this month, take a moment to pause, quiet yourself, and invite God to unfold His Christmas love story to you each day of this month. Ask Him to show you all the beautiful threads woven through each day that demonstrate how much He loves you. May this story captivate and intrigue you with awe and wonder, touching your heart and inspiring you to share that same love with others this season.

✳ ✳ ✳

Dear God,

Thank You for Your great love for me and this world. I ask that You would show me how You are displaying Your great love this Christmas. May I see the Christmas story of Jesus in a new way and may I then share that message of love with others.

Amen

DECEMBER 2

Why *a* Savior?

*So all this was done that it might be fulfilled
which was spoken by the Lord through the prophet, saying:
"Behold, the virgin shall be with child, and bear a Son, and they
shall call His name Immanuel," which is translated,
"God with us." Then Joseph, being aroused from sleep, did as
the angel of the Lord commanded him and took to him his wife,
and did not know her till she had brought forth her firstborn Son.
And he called His name Jesus.*
—MATTHEW 1:22-25

*I call heaven and earth as witnesses today against you,
that I have set before you life and death,
blessing and cursing; therefore choose life,
that both you and your descendants may live.*
—DEUTERONOMY 30:19

*For God did not send His Son into the world to condemn the
world, but that the world through Him might be saved.*
—JOHN 3:17

When I was 16 years old, I thought I had life by the horns. I decided to leave home, move to another state, and live with some friends. I devastated my mom and almost ruined my life. In a matter of a few months, I was kicked out of my friend's house, totaled my car, ran away from the next home, and started dating a guy four years older than me. Even though I thought I was a great Christian girl, a friend had to tell me that I was destroying my life and that I was a bad example to those around me. I was truly blinded and deceived.

My friend's words helped me see the truth that I truly needed a savior. One of the greatest questions we could ever ask ourselves is why did Jesus come to earth as a baby born in Bethlehem, live as a man, and die on a cross for the people of this world? Unless we ask this question, we may never understand the beautiful reason for Christmas nor see our great need for a Messiah, a Savior.

God is the God of the universe. He is perfect, lovely, all that is pure, true, wise, and holy. He has given mankind a choice to enjoy a relationship with Him or they can go their own way and live as if they are their own god. We are not perfect people—we cannot redeem or save ourselves from the cost of our imperfections. Because mankind tends to choose their own way and then fall down, God sent His only perfect son, Jesus, to pay the price for us. No longer do we have to strive, offer sacrifices, and live under the curses of our imperfections and our sins. We now have freedom from that price because Jesus came to earth. Jesus walked in our shoes as a man and gave His perfect life for us so we could experience freedom and a life loved by God. God so loved us that He gave the best sacrifice He had, which was His Son, so that He could gain so many more sons and daughters in us.

Today, I know that Christmas means so much more than just great food, a nativity set, or festive music. It represents Jesus coming to earth bringing true hope, freedom, and salvation from the darkness of this world. It means we have been adopted and made a son or daughter of the most high King of the universe. It means we are never alone, never forgotten, and never abandoned—for He is always with us. This Christmas season, if you receive Him as your Father and Savior, He will receive you. You can invite Him into your life by simply asking Jesus to be your King, Savior, and friend.

✳ ✳ ✳

Dear God,

Thank you for wanting me as your child and friend. Thank you for being with me every moment of every day. I choose You as my King, Savior, father, and friend. Please forgive me for my sin that separates us, and make me clean by Your Son Jesus' perfect sacrifice on the cross. I am now Yours and I choose to draw closer to You each day so that I may know Your love for me fully.

Amen

DECEMBER 3

The Stage *is* Set

And it came to pass in those days that a decree went out from Caesar Augustus that all the world should be registered. This census first took place while Quirinius was governing Syria. So all went to be registered, everyone to his own city. Joseph also went up from Galilee, out of the city of Nazareth, into Judea, to the city of David, which is called Bethlehem, because he was of the house and lineage of David, to be registered with Mary, his betrothed wife, who was with child.
—LUKE 2:1-5

*He has made everything beautiful in its time.
Also He has put eternity in their hearts, except that no one can find out the work that God does from beginning to end.*
—ECCLESIASTES 3:11

*I am the Alpha and the Omega,
the Beginning and the End, the First and the Last.*
—REVELATION 22:13

One Christmas my husband took me to see *The Nutcracker* ballet. What amazing effort and creativity went into bringing this ballet to life for the audience. From the beautiful music to the colorful props, to the perfect timing of every dance—it flowed so beautifully. However, the story of Christmas isn't a sweet story for a musical or a fairy tale or just a great historical event. This story is a beautiful combination of God's meticulous preparation, creativity, and the fulfillment of ancient prophecies, culminating in the arrival of the Savior of the world at the perfect time and place, to bring about the perfect redemption of humanity.

The world at the time of Jesus's birth was in disarray. Herod, a sinister tyrant, was ruling the Jews. They had walked away from God and were now living sinful lives. A time of hopelessness was at hand and many had lost sight of God's promise to bring a Messiah.

But, hope was not lost! God was working! He was building the set, arranging the right people, creating the script, composing the music, and setting the stage. He chose Joseph, from the family of King David, to raise Jesus. He chose Mary, who had a willing and obedient heart even in the face of shame and persecution. He chose an innkeeper to house the king of the universe in a small stable room where animals lived. He chose the setting of Bethlehem, which means "House of Bread," because He knew Jesus would be the Bread of Life to all the world. God wrote beautiful music for angels to sing that filled the sky for shepherds to hear. He put a star in the sky that spoke to specific wise men, who began their journey from Egypt at just the right time, with preordained gifts. They followed the star which led them to the house of Jesus. And in all this, God fulfilled many Bible prophecies written hundreds of years before that predicted the birth of Jesus. Wow, what an amazing composition of God's great love and power all created for us!

God is also writing your story. He is bringing in all the right people, taking you to the right places, creating beautiful music inside you, and scripting each one of your days—all to create your beautiful story. He may seem quiet at times or you may not understand the trials of life, but know He is working it all for your good. He is orchestrating your life to create a beautiful story of His love and purpose for you. This Christmas, may you see the story of Christmas as God's great gesture of love for you. May His love wrap around you today as you allow His story to come alive in your heart. May the story also encourage you that He is turning your story into something beautiful.

Father God,

Thank you for creating the beautiful story of Jesus coming to earth so that I and the world may see Your love for us. Please open my eyes this Christmas season so that I may see You in each day and in each situation. Thank you for filling my story with beauty, purpose, love and more of You.

Amen

DECEMBER 4

Captivated *by* Christmas

Immediately his mouth was opened and his tongue loosed, and he spoke, praising God. Then fear came on all who dwelt around them; and all these sayings were discussed throughout all the hill country of Judea. And all those who heard them kept them in their hearts, saying, "What kind of child will this be?" And the hand of the Lord was with him. Now his father Zacharias was filled with the Holy Spirit, and prophesied, saying: "Blessed is the Lord God of Israel, for He has visited and redeemed His people, And has raised up a horn of salvation for us In the house of His servant David,
—LUKE 1:64

God performs wonders that cannot be fathomed, and miracles that cannot be counted.
—JOB 5:9

With our eyes filled each day with images and messages from our phones, TV, and the world around us, we often miss the beauty of Christmas. We walk by nativity sets with baby Jesus and hear Christmas carols telling of His majesty, but we can be numb to these familiar sights and lose the ability for our hearts to be captivated. Unfortunately, familiarity is the thief of beauty and wonder.

Zechariah, one of the first people mentioned in Luke's account of the Christmas story, was much like us. For him, the Christmas story began in his own home with people he knew. From the time he was a young boy, Zechariah had heard of a Messiah coming to save his people. He also had heard of many miraculous stories from the Jewish writings about Moses, Abraham, and Jacob who knew God and saw the impossible happen. Yet, when an angel appeared to Zechariah and told him of his own miracle—how a child was to be born to him and his wife—he didn't believe it was possible. He was familiar with miracles, but did not recognize his own. Even his name, Zechariah, means "God remembers His promises."

God had remembered His promise to His people to bring a Messiah—a Redeemer, to rescue them, breaking the curse and the power of sin and death. Not only that, He also invited Zechariah to be part of its incredible fulfillment. Like Zechariah, God wants to include us in His story of love and redemption. This Christmas, may you quiet yourself enough to ask, "how has my life become so familiar, so normal, so mundane that I doubt God's love and power to work in me? Today, take a moment to remember—and even jot down—that God has not forgotten you. An angel called Him "Immanuel," which means God is with us. Know that He is with you and loves you so much. He hears you and is working on your behalf, even when it may not seem that way. Ask Him to restore a wonder in your heart of who He is. Ask for eyes to see how you are included in His story of love for the world this Christmas. He knows you. He is with you. He is still doing miracles and He can do them for you.

✳ ✳ ✳

Father God,

Thank You that you want to include me in Your story, for partnering with me to not only do miracles in my life, but enabling me to be a blessing in other people's lives as well. Please help me to see that You are working in my life and show me how I can be the hands and feet of Your love towards others.

Amen

DECEMBER 5

What's *in a* Name?

*And she will bring forth a Son, and you shall call His name
Jesus, for He will save His people from their sins.*
—MATTHEW 1:21-23

*Nor is there salvation in any other, for there is no other name
under heaven given among men by which we must be saved.*
—ACTS 4:12

*And these signs will follow those who believe: In My name
they will cast out demons; they will speak with new tongues;*
—MARK 16:17

When you think of names such as Billy Graham, Gandhi, Martin Luther King, and Mother Teresa—a flood of thoughts rush in about their profound impact on the world. One name can carry immense meaning and power and purpose in people's lives. In biblical times, a person's name could symbolize who that person was or what they were called to do. My name, Leah, means "ruler" or "one who ascends." My last name, Levine, means "beloved" or "one who comes beside." Within the story of Christmas, there is one name that didn't just transform a city or a moment—it changed everything.

Hundreds of years before the Christmas story unfolded, the prophet Isaiah foretold the coming of the Messiah, who would enter the world to save humanity. He said his Name would be called, "Wonderful Counselor," "Mighty God," "Everlasting Father," and "Prince of Peace." In Matthew 1 of the Christmas story, the angel tells Joseph to name the baby "Jesus"—because He will save His people from their sins. The name Jesus, derived from the Hebrew form Yeshua, means "Messiah" or "Savior."

The name of Jesus has been the most powerful, but also the most hated name in all of history from the moment He was born until today. This one name has caused nations to change, families to unite, the sick to be healed, and hurting people to be set free. It has also caused division and wars by those who hate it. This name has caused blind eyes to open and the dead to come to life, but it has also divided countries and people groups because they wanted its glory. The Bible says that even the demons are subject to Jesus' name. It says there is no other name under Heaven by which people can be saved from sin. This one name redeems mankind and holds the heavens in place. The name of Jesus heals every sickness and breaks the power of darkness. I encourage you this Christmas to know Jesus and speak His name over every area of your life. When you speak His name, you are speaking the name of the Wonderful Counselor, the Mighty God, your Everlasting Father, your Prince of Peace, your protector, your Provider, your Savior. In His name, Jesus, all darkness has to flee. Just say the name of Jesus!

***

Father God,

Thank you for sending Your son, Jesus, to be my Savior and Redeemer. Thank you that His name is above every name. And Jesus, I speak Your name into my family, my home, my life, and everywhere I go. I thank you that when I am afraid, sick, hurt, or needing a friend—I can speak Your name and You are there with me and all that I need.

Amen

DECEMBER 6

Favor *with* God

---

*And having come in, the angel said to her,
"Rejoice, highly favored one, the Lord is with you; blessed
are you among women!" But when she saw him, she was
troubled at his saying, and considered what manner of greeting
this was. Then the angel said to her, "Do not be afraid, Mary,
for you have found favor with God."*
—LUKE 1:28

*For I know the thoughts that I think toward you,
says the Lord, thoughts of peace and not of evil, to give you
a future and a hope. Then you will call upon Me and
go and pray to Me, and I will listen to you.*
—JEREMIAH 29:11 -11

The period of time in which Jesus was born is very similar to the world we live in today. Leaders were corrupt, people were harsh with each other, and loving God was not popular. The society Jesus was born into was deeply rooted in an honor/shame culture where you were either honored for who you were or shamed for who you were not. Mary, an ordinary young lady, was engaged to a man named Joseph from the family line of King David. They were not yet married when an angel visited her and told her she would have a baby and he would be the king of the world. Reading about this sounds amazing, but to Mary, an unmarried woman, she knew this meant she would experience shame and persecution. In those days, if a young woman became pregnant without being married, she could be thrown out of her family or even stoned to death. Mary knew she would never live a normal life again. However, Mary did not focus on the ridicule of others, the potential shame, or bad looks she might receive. She had found favor with God and that was the only thing that mattered to her. She received the words of the angel and received it with wonder, thanksgiving, and expectation. And because of her heart to love God in the face of persecution, she went on to be remembered throughout all of history as the mother of Jesus.

During this Christmas season, may you trust that God is doing something great in you and through you even when you feel ordinary. May you not allow the negative and belittling voices you hear each day to cultivate doubt and discouragement in your heart. May you know that with God, nothing is impossible. Despite life being hard or crazy at times, He is still able to touch your heart and do miracles in your life. But like Mary, it all starts with trusting Him, believing He has good for you, and then turning your heart to Him in thankfulness that He is doing what He said He would do. May you say today, "Nothing is impossible for You God, please work in and through me because I am saying 'yes' to You." Then may you watch as God does the impossible through you because you have favor with Him!

✳ ✳ ✳

Father God,

I am not capable of changing the whole world, but I can impact those that are around me. I look to You and say Yes! Yes to Your purpose and plan for my life, Yes to keep my eyes on you even when it doesn't make sense or seems crazy. Yes to how You see me and not how I see myself. In my Yes, I know I will find You, Your favor, Your love, Your miracles, and Your heart for those around me because You love me.

Amen

DECEMBER 7

What Record *is* Playing *in* Your Head?

*And all those who heard it marveled at those things
which were told them by the shepherds. But Mary kept
all these things and pondered them in her heart.*
—LUKE 2:18-19

*Blessed is the man who walks not in the counsel of the ungodly,
nor stands in the path of sinners, nor sits in the seat of the
scornful; But his delight is in the law of the Lord, And in His law
he meditates day and night. He shall be like a tree planted by the
rivers of water, that brings forth its fruit in its season, whose leaf
also shall not wither; and whatever he does shall prosper.*
—PSALM 1:1-3

At Christmas time when I was a little girl, my mom would put a stack of records on our stereo, and the record player would play Christmas songs. One of my favorites was *Elvis' Christmas Album*[1] and my sister and I would sing along as if we were singing with Elvis himself. This was back in the day when it was so cool—at least we thought it was—to have a record player, shag carpet, and velvet curtains. Our record player had this great feature that allowed you to play a record on repeat over and over again. We did this to the point that my mom would tell us to change the record.

Interestingly, our mind has a record player built into it as well. Sometimes it plays great songs that are beautiful and encouraging; other times the record seems to get stuck on repeat, playing songs that are negative and discouraging. In Luke 2, the Bible says that after many glorious things happened to Mary—including angel visitations, Jesus' birth, and prophecy coming to life—she stopped and pondered all these things in her heart. The word "ponder" there means "to hold dear," "to treasure," "to give careful thought," "to think about it over and over." Mary didn't dwell on all the other messages in her head about fear, failure, and what-ifs—even though I am sure there were many. She kept the record playing in her head of all the wondrous things that God had just told her and done in her life.

This Christmas season, will you take a look at what record is playing in your head? Is it a record called *Discouragement*, *Defeat*, or *Not Good Enough*? If so, take that record off the player and put on a new record called *Loved, Hopeful, Beloved of God*, and *God is Doing Something Great*! Take the story of Christmas and how much God loves you and how He is still doing miracles and let it play over and over in your head until it becomes so real to you. Take these promises from the Bible that say God will never leave you, He loves you and calls you His child, and let them play in your mind over and over again. Meditate on them. Write them down. Read them a few times a day until those words gets stuck in your head. Allow the life-giving words and love of God to be the record that is playing on repeat. Then share those same words of hope to those around you this Christmas.

✳ ✳ ✳

Father,

Thank You that You sing a song of hope, love, and victory over me each day. I ask that you help me keep my mind from self-defeating thoughts or words of hopelessness because they are not from you. Help me to cling to the fact that you are with me and speak words of life over me. The Bible says to take my thoughts captive and that my tongue has the power of life or death. Help me to keep my thoughts on you. Help me to use my mouth to speak life not only over myself, but over others as well.

Amen

DECEMBER 8

Community Brings Life

Now Mary arose in those days and went into the hill country with haste, to a city of Judah, and entered the house of Zacharias and greeted Elizabeth. And it happened, when Elizabeth heard the greeting of Mary, that the babe leaped in her womb; and Elizabeth was filled with the Holy Spirit. Then she spoke out with a loud voice and said, "Blessed are you among women, and blessed is the fruit of your womb! But why is this granted to me, that the mother of my Lord should come to me? For indeed, as soon as the voice of your greeting sounded in my ears, the babe leaped in my womb for joy. Blessed is she who believed, for there will be a fulfillment of those things which were told her from the Lord."

—LUKE 1:39-45

The Christmas story is a beautiful story of God's heart to redeem mankind. But many times when we read this story, we read right past many of the amazing characters to only focus on Jesus, the wise men, or Mary. However, God still writes beautiful stories that include normal people like you and me. He desires to include us in the amazing work He wants to do in this world. Continuing on in the Christmas story, we see in Luke 1 that Mary is pregnant with baby Jesus and has left her home to visit a family member named Elizabeth. Being pregnant for the first time Mary may have felt scared and uncertain, especially since she was young and under criticism for being pregnant. I am sure Mary longed for someone safe and wise to talk to. Elizabeth was also pregnant, but much older than Mary. When Mary greeted Elizabeth, the baby in Elizabeth's womb jumped upon hearing Mary's voice. Then Elizabeth was filled with the Holy Spirit and began to praise God. Elizabeth also spoke life and purpose over Mary, which Mary needed. Because of this powerful time together, Elizabeth's son, John, went on to be a champion telling the world about Jesus. What a special time they had together! They needed each other and the encouragement.

God made us to be with people, to have family, to live in community with each other. God did not mean for us to do life alone, especially at Christmas. This season may you know that not only do you play an important part in God's story for this world, but you can also pour value into and encourage the people around you who are all a part of His story. May you celebrate the people around you as Elizabeth celebrated Mary. May you encourage others to link arms in community so they can do life together well.

When we honor each other, the power of the Holy Spirit comes and God's presence becomes real. Oh what our world would look like if we honored and loved each other with all our heart! God wants to create a beautiful story through us. When we let Him, people will see God's love and our stories will change the world in a beautiful way!

✼ ✼ ✼

Father,

You have placed people all around me that I can love, encourage, and show who you are by being an example of You. Please fill me with your Holy Spirit so that I may know how to love well, even know how to love challenging people, and how to be Jesus to people I come in contact with. Please send me to the right places and to the right people at the right time. Send people to encourage me and love me as well. Write Your story through my life!

Amen

DECEMBER 9

You Have *a* Purpose

---

*For he will be great in the sight of the Lord,
and shall drink neither wine nor strong drink. He will also be
filled with the Holy Spirit, even from his mother's womb. And he
will turn many of the children of Israel to the Lord their God.
He will also go before Him in the spirit and power of Elijah,
"to turn the hearts of the fathers to the children," and
the disobedient to the wisdom of the just, to make
ready a people prepared for the Lord."*
—LUKE 1:15-17

*"The Spirit of the Lord is upon Me, Because He has anointed
Me to preach the gospel to the poor; He has sent Me to heal the
brokenhearted, to proclaim liberty to the captives and recovery of
sight to the blind, To set at liberty those who are oppressed;
To proclaim the acceptable year of the Lord."*
—LUKE 4:18-20

Heroes fill the scenes of many of our TV shows and movies. From Superman to Firefighters to secret agents, movies celebrate the rescuer as the hero. God created the greatest hero story when He sent His son Jesus to rescue the world from sin. Yet, unlike Hollywood movies, the main character is not the only person God deems important. In Luke 1, we see John, Jesus' cousin, called to the spotlight. He is given the important role of preparing the world for Jesus. He was called a prophet of the Most High God, his role was to prepare the people for the coming of the Messiah and he preached about God's final judgment calling the people to repent and be baptized. Wow, what a calling! There were many others in the Christmas story who were just normal people like you and me that God gave a special purpose to fulfill. They were not born into royalty or riches, yet God used them to accomplish His story of changing the world.

Do you know that Jesus has a calling on your life as well? Because of the Christmas story, we have a Savior, a Redeemer, and a King and His story continues. He calls us to walk beside Him in His great story. He is still speaking love, wisdom, and power over His people while revealing to us that we have value and purpose in this world.

The Christmas season is such a special time when people's hearts soften and they are willing to listen to the story of baby Jesus. I encourage you to know that you are called, like John and so many others, to speak of God's love and saving power. You are called to tell people how God can heal them and set them free. Even if you are shy or don't like to talk to people, you can send a card, write a note, or even text someone to say that God is with them this Christmas and loves them dearly. Like when Jesus was born in Bethlehem, our world is a lonely and dark place. People need to see the light, love, and peace that comes from knowing Him. You can be a modern-day hero heralding in the good news of Jesus, the Savior of the world. God loves you and wants to empower you with His Spirit to make a difference today. Take the verses at the beginning of the chapter and pray them over yourself and see how God empowers you to make the Christmas story real to someone today!

✳ ✳ ✳

Father,

I ask you to show me the purpose You have for my life. Fill me with vision, understanding, and strength to go forward each day. Help me to show people your goodness and bring them into Your loving arms. Help me to speak Your word to others. May I know that You are with me every step of the way bringing me victory and joy.

Amen

DECEMBER 10

Ordinary *to* Extraordinary

But while he thought about these things, behold, an angel of the Lord appeared to him in a dream, saying, "Joseph, son of David, do not be afraid to take to you Mary your wife, for that which is conceived in her is of the Holy Spirit. And she will bring forth a Son, and you shall call His name Jesus, for He will save His people from their sins." So all this was done that it might be fulfilled which was spoken by the Lord through the prophet...
—LUKE 1:20-22

For you created my inmost being; you knit me together in my mother's womb. I praise you because I am fearfully and wonderfully made; your works are wonderful, I know that full well. My frame was not hidden from you when I was made in the secret place, when I was woven together in the depths of the earth. Your eyes saw my unformed body; all the days ordained for me were written in your book before one of them came to be. How precious to me are your thoughts, God! How vast is the sum of them!
—PSALM 139:13-17

One of the greatest women in my life is my mom. She is a beautiful person inside and out. But to the world's standards, she is ordinary—not special, not highly skilled, or greatly educated. She doesn't have a big following on social media, nor would many people recognize her name. She went to school through the 9th grade and had to drop out at age 14 when she became pregnant. Despite being hurt and misunderstood by so many, my mom never gives up on or stops loving people. This "ordinary" woman impacts more lives on a daily basis than anyone else I know. She is an extraordinary woman to her neighbors, her family, the single moms, and the widows. She was even giving to the nurses she met in the hospital when her husband pass away. She has saved marriages, saved lives, imparted wisdom, and provided for people who had nothing. She is a widow working a part-time job, but gives in a very full-time way. She is truly extraordinary!

Mary and Joseph were the same way. There was nothing special about them. They were just ordinary people living ordinary lives. But when God presented them with a task and a purpose, they did not look at their wallets, their titles, or their popularity—they just said "Yes!" They said yes knowing that what God was asking of them would make them look crazy and foolish. But because they said yes to God's great invitation, He used two ordinary people to birth the Savior of the world. Now that is extraordinary!

The Bible shows us all throughout its pages that God uses ordinary people and makes them extraordinary. God has always loved to work through and bless people who will say yes to Him. You don't have to be famous, exceptionally talented, or physically beautiful for God to use you to change the world. He asked Mary and Joseph to go against the norms of society and be subjected them to shaming from their community. Their obedience meant that Mary had to travel for many days, pregnant, and most likely uncomfortably sitting on a donkey, to get to Bethlehem for the census. All of these things happened to fulfill the prophecy stating that the Messiah would be born in Bethlehem.

What is God asking you to do this Christmas season? Can you lay aside any voices that tell you you're not good enough? That you are not smart enough? That you don't have extraordinary things to say? Ask your loving Father to reveal to you His heart for you and what He's calling you to do and then say "Yes" to whatever He says. There is a world that is waiting for you to say Yes!

Father,

I praise You that You use ordinary people to do extraordinary things. I ask that you take all that I am and use it to impact the people and places around me. Use my mouth to speak life and my hands to help others. Use my heart to love people well and my resources to help those in need. In all of this, may people see Your love for them through me and may I know Your great love for me.

Amen

DECEMBER 11

He Sees Our Need

---

*He is despised and rejected by men, a Man of sorrows
and acquainted with grief. And we hid, as it were, our faces
from Him; He was despised, and we did not esteem Him.
Surely He has borne our griefs and carried our sorrows;
yet we esteemed Him stricken, smitten by God, and afflicted.
But He was wounded for our transgressions, He was bruised
for our iniquities; the chastisement for our peace was
upon Him, and by His stripes we are healed.*
—ISAIAH 53:3-5

*"Therefore do not be like them. For your Father knows the things
you have need of before you ask Him.*
—MATTHEW 6:8

*And you will seek Me and find Me,
when you search for Me with all your heart.*
—JEREMIAH 29:13

As human beings, we often fall short in caring for one another and upholding what is right. Sometimes it feels like we put small band aids on large problems. We spend money on things that don't matter instead of protecting children or saving lives. Instead of walking with someone through a hard time, we may selfishly choose to not answer the phone. Instead of giving, teaching, and helping those who struggle—we just label them less fortunate.

God saw our need for help, healing, love, and salvation. But in His great love and wisdom, He didn't give us a program, a three-step plan, a pep talk, or an institution to govern us. No, He saw our great need to be rescued from death and gave us Himself. He gave us His Son, Jesus, who embodies all that we need to have life. Jesus is true peace. He is health and healing. He is redemption and forgiveness from sin. He is provision for all that we need. He is life and freedom. Jesus is our Savior, friend, and comforter. He is all we need. To me, one of the most beautiful parts of the Christmas story is that the God of the universe sent His only Son to be born to ordinary people, in an ordinary town, and to be born in a very ordinary and lowly room. God made sure that Jesus walked as we walk and that He understood our sorrows, struggles, and questions. Jesus wasn't born in an earthly palace to a king where He would experience a privileged life and not be able to relate to us. No, God sent Jesus to humanity in the most humble way—to be born in a messy, stinky room, and to be laid in a feeding trough called a manger.

God gave us His best so He could reach us at our worst. Jesus meets us where we are no matter where that may be and no matter how messy it may look. He is all that we need. He is our hope for a future and our companion who never leaves us. Today, I encourage you to look at the nativity scene again. Look at the manger and know that God cares and came down to walk with you. He loves you, hears you, knows how you feel, and has lived a hard life here on earth as well. He can relate to you. He can meet your every need, whether mental, physical, emotional, or spiritual. He wants to give you His perfect love. Just ask Him today to take the cares in your heart and the needs in your hands. It is His joy to love you and be your Savior.

※ ※ ※

Father,

Thank you that you did not come to earth as a baby born in a palace or into a life of ease. Thank you for coming to earth and living a normal life. Thank you for knowing what it feels like to hurt, to struggle, to be in pain, to feel rejected, and to feel hungry. I ask you today to be so near to me. I give you my heart and my needs and ask You to be my bread of life filling every empty area within me. I need you to heal me and make me whole and live inside me.

Amen

DECEMBER 12

Emmanuel, God *with* Us

---

*"Behold, the virgin shall be with child,
and bear a Son, and they shall call His name Immanuel,"
which is translated, "God with us."*
—MATTHEW 1:23

*One thing I have desired of the Lord,
that will I seek:
That I may dwell in the house of the Lord
all the days of my life.
To behold the beauty of the Lord,
and to inquire in His temple.
For in the time of trouble
He shall hide me in His pavilion;
in the secret place of His tabernacle
He shall hide me;
He shall set me high upon a rock.*
—PSALM 27:4-5

> *Therefore the Lord Himself will give you a sign:*
> *Behold, the virgin shall conceive and bear a Son,*
> *and shall call His name Immanuel.*
> —ISAIAH 7:14

When I was a little girl, there were many times of turmoil and strife in my home. It was hard to get away and find a place of peace. But there was one place I loved to go that was peaceful, beautiful, and I could feel God's presence near to me. This place of sanctuary was a small ocean area where my dad would go fishing. As a small girl I would walk along the shore by myself, look at the water, see the colorful seashells, and listen as God used the waves to wash over my heart. I found peace there and God's presence was felt real to me.

In Matthew 2, God also knew Joseph, was in a hard place and needed peace. Joseph loved Mary and was engaged to marry her, but he had received the shocking news that Mary was pregnant knowing that he was not the father of her baby. He was hurt and considered ending the engagement with her. God saw His pain and came near to him, sending him a message. An angel appeared to Joseph and told him to take Mary to be his wife because the baby inside her womb was God's Son, who would be the Savior of the world. He told Joseph to name him "Emmanuel"—which means "God with us."

Joseph had free will and could have said "no" and broken off the engagement to Mary, leaving her on her own. However, God truly became "Emmanuel" to Joseph in that moment. God was near to him—speaking to him while he was confused and hurting—and Joseph said "yes" to God's request.

God knew humanity would continue to choose their own ways over a relationship with Him so He sent His son, Jesus, to this world to restore us to our loving Father. God greatly desires to be with His people so much so that He was willing to give His most prized possession, Jesus, to pay the price that sin requires. Jesus did this on the cross when He died for all of mankind. God offers Himself and the perfect blood of Jesus as a gift to be received. He does not force a relationship upon us. He wants us to freely love Him and freely choose Him.

This Christmas season, let's bring Him your hurt, your pain, and your fear so that you can step into relationship with Him. Quiet yourself enough to come in close to His presence. Ask Him to speak to you. Then be still enough to listen to what He says. May you be mindful not to allow the familiar story of Christmas, the hustle of buying gifts, or the fancy music productions to take the place of you personally preparing room for Him in your heart. His greatest desire and treasure is you. Will you draw near to Him, quiet yourself, and allow Him to be Emmanuel—God with you—in this Christmas season?

Father,

Thank you for offering your perfect son to pay the price for my sin so I could be called Your child again and be so near to You. I pray this Christmas that I will still myself enough to sense your love for me, that I will know a sweet relationship with you, and that I will hear Your heart for me and those around me. I need You more than I need my own ways. Help me to draw near to your perfect presence today.

Amen

DECEMBER 13

Prepare Him Room

---

*And she brought forth her firstborn Son,
and wrapped Him in swaddling cloths, and laid Him in a
manger, because there was no room for them in the inn.*
—LUKE 2:7

*Heal the sick, cleanse the lepers, raise the dead,
cast out demons. Freely you have received, freely give.*
—MATTHEW 10:8

*He who is faithful in what is least is faithful also in much;
and he who is unjust in what is least is unjust also in much.*
—LUKE 16:10

Have you ever seen a nature photo where a tree is growing inside a huge rock or a beautiful flower is blooming in the midst of a waterless desert? It is not only stunning to see but it is also full of wonder to comprehend how it grows and thrives in the midst of barrenness. Many times in life we think if we can just achieve more money, or a better degree, a new friend group, or a new promotion, we will finally thrive or create a meaningful life. Striving to grow and become our best selves is a wonderful pursuit that aligns with God's heart for us. Yet, often we seek opportunities far and wide, overlooking the potential that lies right where we are. Jesus was born not in a palace, despite being a king; not into wealth, even though He owns the world; and not into lavish comfort, even though Heaven is His home. He was born in a basement apartment where animals were lived. He was laid in a feeding trough for His bed since He did not have a cradle. He was born to two common people who were far from the comforts of their humble home. He did this all for us, not so we would look for luxury, or fame, or accolades, but so we would know that we can find Him wherever we are in life.

This Christmas season, cherish the people around you. Show them honor and appreciation. Appreciate the home you have and the meals you enjoy each day. Use the resources and influence you have to encourage and bless those around you. Your kind words today could make a world of difference for a person you encounter this week.

Jesus didn't need perfect conditions to save the world. He only needed to be present and obedient to what God told Him to do. Don't wait until everything is perfectly in place to enjoy life, make a difference, or reach out to meet the needs of others. Use what you have and make it your best. God will multiply your obedience and take your act of love, kindness, or prayer and give it have far-reaching effects. Like that tree thriving on a rock or a flower blooming in the desert embrace life where you are at—even in the midst of your trials, or struggles, or your loneliness. As in the beautiful Christmas hymn, "Joy to the World,"[2] we sing the famous lyrics, "Let every heart prepare Him room, let Heaven and nature sing." Will you prepare Him room in your heart today, right where you are, to move in your life and in the lives of those around you? If you do, you will find Heaven and nature singing with joy for all that God can do through you!

✳ ✳ ✳

Father,

I ask that You help me make the most of where I am at. I know that I don't have to be perfect, just willing to listen to You and willing to do what I hear You say. Help me bloom and grow where you have planted me. Help me to see my blessings and then to bless those around me. Help me know your great love for me so I can love people around me. Fill me to speak Your words of life over those I encounter and help me to reflect your perfect love.

Amen

DECEMBER 14

He Found You

Now there were in the same country shepherds living out in the fields, keeping watch over their flock by night. And behold, an angel of the Lord stood before them, and the glory of the Lord shone around them, and they were greatly afraid. Then the angel said to them, "Do not be afraid, for behold, I bring you good tidings of great joy which will be to all people. For there is born to you this day in the city of David a Savior, who is Christ the Lord. And this will be the sign to you: You will find a Babe wrapped in swaddling cloths, lying in a manger." And suddenly there was with the angel a multitude of the heavenly host praising God and saying: "Glory to God in the highest, And on earth peace, goodwill toward men!"
—LUKE 2:8-14 8

Have you ever had a time when you felt like your life was on repeat and each day was exactly the same? Did it feel like everyone around you was living life to the fullest, while your life felt unimportant, unseen, making you wish you had more purpose. I am sure the shepherds in the Christmas story understood this feeling as well. In Luke 2 the scripture says that outside of Bethlehem, the shepherds were in a field during the night watching their sheep. Let's pause there and think about what their life would have been like. Even though the skies were above them, it was dark, wolves were lurking around trying to get their sheep, and their days and nights were filled with the same thing day in and day out—watching sheep. They may have been bored or lonely. I am sure they felt unimportant—out in the same fields each day with no one around. They had heard the great stories of King David and the promised Messiah. In fact, within God's beautiful narrative and intricate design, it's possible that the field where the shepherds stood once belonged to King David or Boaz, ancestors of Jesus, or that the sheep they were tending were Passover lambs destined to become a sacrifice for the people. But I am sure they did not feel as important as King David or Boaz.

But one night, all that changed. God knew where they were and He included them in the most amazing story of His son. He met them in their day-to-day life and gave them such an important role to play in witnessing Jesus' birth! Luke 2:9 says that all of a sudden, an angel appeared and lit up the sky with the glory of God. It was so brilliant it actually terrified the shepherds. But the angel comforted them, sharing with them the amazing news that Jesus, the Messiah, was born near them in Bethlehem. Their lives went from quiet and unimportant to full of meaning and purpose. The God of the universe found them so valuable that He personally revealed to them the birth of His Son, the long-awaited Messiah. God didn't tell kings or high officials. No, He chose to tell lowly shepherds sitting in a field.

This Christmas, know that God wants to meet you right where you are. He wants to come and fill each day of your life with His love and purpose. He sees and knows you better than you know yourself. You matter to him and He wants to give you value, purpose, and hope. Just as Jesus chose shepherds to demonstrate that He is the Great Shepherd to His people, so you were made in His image to bear His light to those around you. You are seen, you are heard, and you are known so intimately by the God of the Christmas story!

***

Father God,

Thank you that there is not a place I can go that you cannot find me there. Even now, You are with me and long to show me Your love. Please put Your value, purpose, and vision in my heart. Help me to know that You are with me every second of every day. Help me to bring that same value and love to those around me today, in Jesus name.

Amen

DECEMBER 15

Finding Treasure

When they heard the king, they departed; and behold, the star which they had seen in the East went before them, till it came and stood over where the young Child was. When they saw the star, they rejoiced with exceedingly great joy. And when they had come into the house, they saw the young Child with Mary His mother, and fell down and worshiped Him. And when they had opened their treasures, they presented gifts to Him: gold, frankincense, and myrrh.
—MATTHEW 2:9-11

*The multitude of camels shall cover your land,
the dromedaries of Midian and Ephah;
all those from Sheba shall come;
they shall bring gold and incense,
and they shall proclaim the praises of the Lord.*
—ISAIAH 60:6

*But without faith it is impossible to please Him,
for he who comes to God must believe that He is,
and that He is a rewarder of those who diligently seek Him.*
—HEBREWS 11:6

Treasure hunting has always intrigued me. With an ancient map, a captivating story, and tools for the journey, there is the possibility of finding an amazing treasure. The story of the Wise Men in the story of Christmas reminds me of treasure hunters. These men were neither raised Jewish nor were they local to Bethlehem so would not have heard the rumor of a special baby who had been born there. They did not know Mary and Joseph or hear the words given to them by the angel. No, these men were wealthy scholars from the East, possibly Iran, Iraq or Saudi Arabia, which are countries far from Bethlehem. They were very wealthy and respected men who studied history, the skies, and searched the stars for prophecies and omens. They were foreigners who had their own king. What set them apart is that they were watching the sky and saw the sign of the star.

The Wise Men lived in times much like ours. Many Bible scholars believe they probably came from the ancient country of Persia, hundreds of miles away. If so, they may have become familiar with the Old Testament prophecies about the coming Messiah through Jews who were forced to settle there centuries before. Jewish people like the prophet, Daniel, were enslaved and forced into other lands. They may have heard of the Jewish prophecy of Micah, which said out of Bethlehem a king would come who would save his people. These Wise Men journeyed many days from the East to the West with a large caravan of people and costly gifts following the star to a specific place in Bethlehem. These men were determined to find this King they had heard about so they could worship him. They came with gifts of gold which was a gift fit for a king. They brought gifts of frankincense which was used in the offering of sacrifices and used in worship which acknowledged Jesus as Priest. They brought him Myrrh, which was a burial spice, showing not only their willingness to leave their past homeland and their old ways, but also symbolized the death of Jesus on the cross that would bring life to the world.

This Christmas season are you ready to look for Jesus and leave your past behind? What thoughts might be holding you back from going after God? I encourage you to rise up, lift up your eyes, and follow His leading. Bring your gifts of praise and adoration to Jesus your King. Bring your heart and life because He has saved you from sin and the powers of this world. Bring the offering of your gifts and talents and leave the past behind, determining to never go back. When the Wise Men found Jesus it changed their lives forever. They even had an encounter with an angel who spoke to the them telling them to go home a different way. God is ready to encounter you today and transform the course of your destiny—if only you will let go of your old ways and set your course to find Him!

Father,

Today, I choose to listen to You even when the messages around me and the things I see can bring me down. I choose to search your Word for hope and truth until I find You and Your love for me. Help me to speak life to those around me and encourage them with Your message of hope this Christmas season. Thank You that in You is perfect hope and love.

Amen

DECEMBER 16

From Death *to* Life

---

*And behold, there was a man in Jerusalem whose
name was Simeon, and this man was just and devout, waiting
for the Consolation of Israel, and the Holy Spirit was upon him.
And it had been revealed to him by the Holy Spirit that he would
not see death before he had seen the Lord's Christ. So he came by
the Spirit into the temple. And when the parents brought in the
Child Jesus, to do for Him according to the custom of the law,
he took Him up in his arms and blessed God and said:*

*"Lord, now You are letting Your servant depart in peace,
According to Your word;
For my eyes have seen Your salvation
Which You have prepared before the face of all peoples,
A light to bring revelation to the Gentiles,
and the glory of Your people Israel."*
—LUKE 2:25-32

*"Most assuredly, I say to you, he who hears My word and believes
in Him who sent Me has everlasting life, and shall not come
into judgment, but has passed from death into life.*
—JOHN 5:24

The thief does not come except to steal, and to kill, and to destroy.
I have come that they may have life, and that
they may have it more abundantly.
—JOHN 10:10

There was a song that debuted in 2006 by John Mayer called "Waiting on the World to Change."³ This was a very popular song and reflected the heart cry of that generation. All too often it feels like we are waiting on the world to change for the better. This is how Simeon and Anna felt in Luke 2. Simeon was a well-respected, godly man. Anna was a woman who prayed and knew God's voice. They both knew the scriptures telling of a Messiah who would come and bring salvation and hope. The world they lived in looked much like ours does today— turmoil, wars, corrupt leaders, and perverse people. They were waiting and praying for their world to change. They were waiting for God to send His savior to bring healing to their land.

The Bible says that Mary and Joseph took Jesus to the temple in Jerusalem to dedicate Him to God. When they arrived, the first person they met was a man named Simeon. Simeon's name means "God has heard." When Simeon saw Jesus, he took Him in his arms and praised God. He said, "My eyes have seen Your salvation…" God was letting His people know that He had heard their cry and He had sent His salvation through Jesus. The next person Mary and Joseph encounter at the temple was Anna. Her name means "grace," "favor," and "beauty." She also praised God and was rejoicing as she met the baby Jesus knowing that He was the rescuer, the redeemer the world had been waiting for. God was revealing to His people that Jesus came to redeem us from sin, from the curse of the Old Testament law, and from ourselves. Jesus is grace, He shows us favor, and He changes us within. This Christmas season, God has heard our cry, paid our price for sin, and covered us with His beautiful grace through Jesus. As you celebrate the season with family or friends or even just by yourself, know that God has heard your cry. He wants to give you life—turn shame to beauty, loneliness to belonging, religious works to a relationship with Him. You may feel like you have been waiting forever to see things in your world change. But know this one thing, God had heard all of Simeon and Anna's prayers. Even though it may have taken a few years, the fulfillment of their prayers came from seeing that the Messiah had come to earth to fulfill God's plan of redemption.

Instead in their old age, the fulfillment of their prayers was seeing that the Messiah Jesus had come to earth to fulfill God's plan of redemption. Will you allow Him to do the same for you today? Find Jesus this Christmas season. Find Him in the midst of your situations and days. We are not promised an easy life, but we are promised that He will never leave us, that He will give us victory, and that He will help us each day. Know that He came to be with you, to have a deep and personal relationship with you, and to above all to bring you life!

Father,

God thank You for sending Jesus to this world for me.
Thank You that Your Christmas story demonstrates that You went to people, meeting them right where they were at, and showed them that they were valued and important. Help me to feel valued and important to You. Help me to feel Your love, purpose, and hope today. Help me to let go of my fears and know that You are alive.

Amen

DECEMBER 17

The Greatest Gift

For unto us a Child is born,
Unto us a Son is given;
And the government will be upon His shoulder.
And His name will be called
Wonderful, Counselor, Mighty God,
Everlasting Father, Prince of Peace.
Of the increase of His government and peace
There will be no end,
Upon the throne of David and over His kingdom,
To order it and establish it with judgment and justice
From that time forward, even forever.
The zeal of the Lord of hosts will perform this.
—ISAIAH 9:6-7

Why are you cast down, O my soul?
And why are you disquieted within me?
Hope in God, for I shall yet praise Him.
For the help of His countenance.
—PSALM 42:5

At Christmas time, my family enjoys a few beloved traditions. On Christmas morning, we stay in our pajamas, watch a Christmas parade on TV, and eat a big breakfast. Then we all plop ourselves on the couches with the Bible to read the Christmas story from the book of Luke. After the story, we each tell of what God has done for us that year and pray for each other. My kids open their presents, saving the gift I mark as special—being the greatest in value—as the last gift they open.

God did the same thing for us as well. He gave us the gift of His presence in the Garden of Eden. Then He gave us His word to help us know how to live and keep us from sin. He also gave us His Spirit to live inside us. But the greatest gift He has given us is Jesus. Isaiah 9:6-7 tells us why Jesus is the greatest gift. The scripture starts out by saying that the government shall be upon His shoulders. This is our hope that no matter what government is ruling in our land, we still have a greater King who leads us, loves us, and is more powerful than any human leader. Next, the scripture identifies him by four names.

First, His name is Wonderful Counselor. God knew we would need His counsel, His guidance, and His care to help us make it through each day. Secondly, His name is Mighty God. Jesus's mighty power broke the power of death and sin off of our lives when He destroyed them at the cross. His great power is still working on our behalf today. Thirdly, He is called Everlasting Father. When Jesus died on the cross, He made it possible for us to be welcomed into His family, giving us full access to the throne of God, and calling us children of God. What a wonderful feeling to know I am God's child, and I am not abandoned or left alone anymore! I am called His beloved. And lastly, Jesus is the Prince of Peace. In a world that knows very little peace, I am so thankful that Jesus is my peace and the One who calms the storms inside me.

Finally, scripture talks about the eternal reign of King Jesus. Leaders, kings, and rulers will come and go in this world, but the reign of Jesus will never end. His kingship is marked by righteousness, purity, justice, love, and peace. Wow, that is my King! This Christmas season, take these two verses in Isaiah and read them a few times to soak in the message that Jesus is our greatest gift. He is the gift that keeps on giving and never ends. He is the gift that doesn't grow old, doesn't go out of style, doesn't break, or lose value. He is all that we need if we will receive Him as our greatest gift this Christmas!

Father,

In Jesus' great name and because of what He did on the cross, I receive Your peace, Your comfort, Your counsel, Your forgiveness, Your power, and I know that I am Your beloved child. Help me to focus on who You are and all that You have done for me. May this message speak louder in my heart and mind than the messages of the world.

Amen!

DECEMBER 18

Defiant Joy

*When they saw the star, they rejoiced
with exceedingly great joy.*
—MATTHEW 2:10

*Then the angel said to them, "Do not be afraid,
for behold, I bring you good tidings of great
joy which will be to all people.*
—LUKE 2:10

*Looking unto Jesus, the author and finisher of our faith,
who for the joy that was set before Him endured the cross,
despising the shame, and has sat down at the
right hand of the throne of God.*
—HEBREWS 12:2

*You will show me the path of life; In Your presence is fullness
of joy; At Your right hand are pleasures forevermore.*
—PSALM 16:11

One of the most popular Christmas songs is "Joy to the World"[4] which was written in 1719 by the English minister and hymnist, Isaac Watts. Even though this song was not originally written as a Christmas carol, it has been adopted as a beloved Christmas song because of the mention of Jesus coming to earth and the joy that He brings the world. All too often we see the joy of Christmas as a feeling that is based on the sounds, smells, and the events of the season. But if you look at the Christmas story in the Bible, the only sounds heard were of animals, a woman giving birth, a baby crying, and an evil king speaking orders to kill the child. The only smells were of straw or hay, dirty clothes from a long journey, and a barn where animals lived. The events happening at that time were a population census people were mandated to attend, a long journey to get to their hometown, and Mary and Joseph not able to find a proper place to sleep.

So where is joy in the true Christmas story and why do we associate joy with a story that does not feel like a joyful Christmas at all? The type of joy that Jesus offers us is not based on a feeling, an event, or even something incredible happening in our life. The type of joy we see in the Christmas story is something that only comes from Jesus and knowing Him. It is not based on our circumstances nor our emotions, it is based on His love, His presence, His promises, and His life living in us.

Bono, of the band U2, refers to it as "defiant joy,"[5] because it defies reasoning. According to C.S. Lewis, "Joy is the serious business of heaven."[6] If God found it so vital to fill the characters in this story with joy, how much more important is it for us to be filled with joy as we go out to the world around us? Christians should have such contagious joy that it makes the world jealous and compels them to seek out the Jesus that lives inside of us. Life will always have trials, sorrows, and pain, but in the midst of these things, we were meant to have joy. Paul said to "consider it pure joy...whenever we experience trials of many kinds."[7] Trials are the opposite of the happiness the world tries to sell us. In the midst of hard things, Jesus will come to fill us with joy—something that cannot be taken from us. Joy is our strength and our hope, because we know that Jesus is king. This Christmas season, choose joy. Ask God to give you overflowing joy and help you to find joy in the little things of life that He has done. You will find a new strength, a new peace, and a new thankfulness for life when you choose joy.

❋ ❋ ❋

Father,

Thank You that Your joy can fill my heart even when the world around me looks dim. Thank You that joy gives me strength and You provide hope to encourage me and me move forward. I ask You Father that You fill me with joy to overflowing until the overflow spills out from me onto those around me. Thank you for putting a new song of joy in my heart and gratitude for who you are and all You have done.

Amen

DECEMBER 19

From Trials *to* Testimonies

*And we know that all things work together for good
to those who love God, to those who are
the called according to His purpose.*
—ROMANS 8:28

*For we do not have a High Priest who cannot sympathize
with our weaknesses, but was in all points tempted
as we are, yet without sin.*
—HEBREWS 4:15

*And they overcame him by the blood of the Lamb,
and by the word of their testimony;
and they loved not their lives unto the death.*
—REVELATIONS 12:11

One Christmas when my kids were very little, we were going through a very hard time, had little money and no heat in our home. We had to wear our jackets in the morning until the kitchen stove had time to warm up the house. During this time, I received a piece of mail showing a picture of a child on the front who was cold and appeared to have no heat as well. I ripped open that envelope and with a moved heart tried to figure out how I could help them. That short trial in my life created a great compassion for those who struggle with poverty.

Have you ever gone through hard seasons in life and looked back to wonder how you made it through? God sent His Son Jesus to us as a human and a baby so He could walk in our shoes. The Bible says in Isaiah 53:3 that Jesus was a man who was "despised and rejected." He was a man of sorrows and acquainted with grief. Jesus knew pain. He knew rejection and abandonment. He felt alone at times and was often misunderstood. Even his friends turned on Him when things got difficult for them. But everything Jesus experienced on earth prepared Him to be the best Savior and King humanity could ever have. In Hebrews 4:15, it tells us that Jesus can sympathize and relate to us because He has endured many trials and struggles just as we have. Winston Churchill, the British statesman, soldier, and writer, was quoted as saying, "To every man there comes in his lifetime that special moment when he is figuratively tapped on the shoulder and offered a chance to do a very special thing, unique to him and fitted to his talents. What a tragedy if that moment finds him unprepared or unqualified for that which would be his finest hour."[8]

I would like to encourage and challenge you to know that everything you have gone through, the good, the bad, and the painful, will all be used to prepare you for the great calling you were created for. It will grow you, strengthen you, give you wisdom, character, and compassion, as well as create in you a preparedness to be able to navigate all areas of life. My mom, who has been through more than most humans would be able to endure, has this saying, "No pain is wasted." She is determined that all that she has gone through will now be used to help others get through hard things in life successfully. She does not want her pain to be wasted. This Christmas season, know that all you have gone through will not be wasted. Take your challenges, your pain, and your fears and give them to Jesus. Just as He transformed the trials of Mary, Joseph, and many more into testimonies, so He will do the same for you. Offer yourself to Him and watch how He uses you to encourage, empower, and love those around you. You have gold inside!

Father God,

Thank You that you can turn anything for my good. Thank You that You are turning my pain into perfect love for others. You are turning my trials into the foundations I need to move forward. I pray for wisdom, guidance, and strength to see things as You see them. Then empower me to help other people see You in the midst of their trials. In Jesus name!

Amen

DECEMBER 20

Knowing Him

*For my eyes have seen Your salvation
Which You have prepared before the face of all peoples,
A light to bring revelation to the Gentiles,
and the glory of Your people Israel."*
—LUKE 2:30-32

*Your word I have hidden in my heart,
That I might not sin against You.
Blessed are You, O Lord!
Teach me Your statutes.
With my lips I have declared
All the judgments of Your mouth.
I have rejoiced in the way of Your testimonies,
As much as in all riches.
I will meditate on Your precepts,
And contemplate Your ways.
I will delight myself in Your statutes;
I will not forget Your word.*
—PSALM 119:11-16

Your word is a lamp to my feet and a light to my path.
—PSALM 119:105

In today's world, it feels like there are countless counterfeits of the real thing—whether it's our currency, the news we consume, or the products we buy. The Federal Reserve, who manages the United States money supply, diligently trains their employees to recognize counterfeit money within a few seconds of looking at a dollar bill. These professionals study the paper texture, the markings, the look, and even the color to know if the bill is real or fake. So how do they know if a dollar is real or a fake? They are required to study a real dollar bill for thousands of hours so they know what it should look like. An employee can detect a fake bill because they truly know the real one.

In the time that Jesus was born, there were many leaders claiming to be the real Messiah or King. Herod, the Roman leader when Jesus was born, was even given the title, King of the Jews—the same title put over Jesus' head at His crucifixion. However, Mary and Joseph knew that the baby Jesus was the real Messiah and so did the shepherds, the Wise men, Simeon, Anna, and many more. Even King Herod knew Jesus was the true Messiah, which is why he felt like Jesus was a threat to his throne and tried to kill him. How did these people, all of different places and backgrounds, know for that Jesus was the true Messiah and King? They all had one thing in common—they knew the scriptures. Each one of them had heard the ancient Hebrew scriptures foretelling of the Messiah being born of a virgin,[9] from the lineage of Judah,[10] and that his birth would be in a specific town—Bethlehem.[11] So when the angel appeared to Mary and Joseph, or the star appeared to the wisemen, or the heavenly hosts appeared to the shepherds telling of this Savior—they knew the prophecies were coming true. Even the Wise Men, who were from the East and not Israelites, had studied the ancient scriptures enough to know of the Jewish Messiah and Jacob's star rising out of Israel.[12]

This Christmas season and even into the new year, I challenge you to dive deep into the Bible and seek to know the God who loves you, the Savior who gave His life for you, and the Holy Spirit who is always with you. Know His heart, His words, His character, so that when confronted with fake people, fake news, wrong beliefs, and the lies the devil loves to tell us, we will recognize the falsehood because we know the real heart of God. From the beginning of time, the devil has tried to convince people to doubt God's words and His heart for them. He uses the same schemes today. Your best defense is to seek God in His word as if you are seeking out hidden gold. Seek Him as if your life depends on it. Seek Him until you find Him; and when you do, it will be the greatest fulfillment of your life and you will find real and authentic treasure.

Father God,

Thank You that Your Word is the truth and life to me. Help me to love Your Word more than any other words, books, and information. Help me to make Your Word the foundation of my life, my heart, and my thoughts. May I live in it each morning and carry it through the day in my heart so it defeats the lies. May Your word live through me in the words I speak to others.

Amen

DECEMBER 21

The Amazing Gift of Hope

*For my eyes have seen Your salvation
Which You have prepared before the face of all peoples,
A light to bring revelation to the Gentiles,
and the glory of Your people Israel.*
—LUKE 2:30-32

*And not only that, but we also glory in tribulations,
knowing that tribulation produces perseverance; and
perseverance, character; and character, hope. Now hope
does not disappoint, because the love of God has been poured out
in our hearts by the Holy Spirit who was given to us.*
—ROMANS 5:4-5

*Why are you cast down, O my soul?
And why are you disquieted within me?
Hope in God;
For I shall yet praise Him,
The help of my countenance and my God.*
—PSALM 42:11

*Now may the God of hope fill you with all joy and peace
in believing, that you may abound in hope
by the power of the Holy Spirit.*
—ROMAN 15:13

Are there ever mornings where staying in bed sounds way better than getting up? Maybe you have a long day of work ahead or you have to face something hard today or maybe it's an average day but you feel you need a day off. There is one thing that gets me out of the bed each morning (besides coffee) and that is *hope*. Webster's Dictionary defines "hope" as a desire with an expectation of fulfillment, a trust, an expectation that something is going to happen. Each person you hear about in the Christmas story, all had their hope and their expectation set on one person—God. They knew that God had promised to send them a Messiah, a Savior to rescue them and to be their King.

Their hope rested in His promise which was very real to them. I am sure it is what gave them strength to keep going in the hard times when evil Rome took over and the persecution of the Jewish people made the times difficult and dark. Their only hope was God—His goodness, and His promises. And because this was their hope when Jesus was born, they knew their hope had arrived and the news was a cause for great rejoicing.

This Christmas season, what have you placed your hope in? Is your hope in the feelings of Christmas or in the magic of the season? Is it in your spouse or friends—hoping they will love you well? Is your hope in your job, your money, or your social following? Maybe your hope is in a dream you want to fulfill, a goal you are close to reaching, a degree you are trying to finish, or a company you want to start. Can I encourage you today to put your hope in the person of Jesus? All the earthly things we put our hope in are not bad things, but they are temporary things. Events end, people let us down, goals are accomplished and become meaningless, and money is fleeting. But Jesus has no beginning or end nor will He ever change. We can pursue and enjoy earthly things, but our Hope must be found in Him. The thing I am so thankful for when I wake up each morning is that I know God is good. He is perfect. He loves me. He is my perfect peace. He is working all things for my good. He is my protection. He is God over this crazy world and He wins in the end. Without this hope, I'm not sure that I would have any reason to get up each morning. Will you set your eyes and your hope on Jesus this Christmas season? His hope does not disappoint!

Father God,

Thank You that You do not change. You are not flaky nor moody. You don't have a bad day and You are not selfish. I choose to put my hope in the God who is faithful, who loves me, and who will move heaven and earth to be with me. Help me to share this hope You have given me with
others today so they can know the real reason for Christmas.

Amen

DECEMBER 22

A Willing Surrender

Then Mary said, "Behold the maidservant of the Lord!
Let it be to me according to your word."
And the angel departed from her.
—LUKE 1:38

Your kingdom come. Your will be done on earth as it is in heaven.
—MATTHEW 6:10

For I have come down from heaven, not to do My own will,
but the will of Him who sent Me.
—JOHN 6:38

I believe there is a beautiful red thread woven through the Christmas story and found all throughout the Bible. This thread is seen in the characters portrayed in each story and the perfect example of this thread is Jesus Himself. So you may ask, what is this scarlet red thread? It is called Surrender.

Hearing the word *surrender*, you may think of some popular war movie where the opposing troops wave a white flag to show their enemy that they giving up and surrendering. Though that is one type of surrender, the surrender I am referring to here is the laying down of your will, the fight against needing things your go your way—a true giving of your life to Jesus. This type of surrender is beautifully seen in the characters of the Christmas story.

In this story, the first surrender doesn't take place in Bethlehem but takes place in Heaven. Jesus, God's Son, willingly accepts God's request for Him to go to earth as in the form of a man, die a sinner's death, rise again, and save humanity from their sin. Jesus willingly surrendered His life and His will. He was obedient to his Father knew this was the only way and that He was the only and was willing to be the perfect sacrifice.

Next, we see Mary surrender her life and her reputation to accept the words of the angel that she will be pregnant with a child to be named Jesus. Mary surrendered her will, her reputation, and her life to obey the call of God on her life. She knew it would mean shame, questions, possible rejection, and pain in her body to deliver a child during childbirth. Not only did Mary surrender to God's words, she praised Him and thanked Him for choosing her. And ever since, her name has been remembered throughout all the world. Joseph chose to surrender to God's plan even though it did not make sense as he would be looked down on for taking Mary to be his wife, when she was already pregnant, and the baby wasn't his son. The shepherds left their flocks behind, surrendering their hearts to go worship a newborn king. The Wise men surrendered their time, their reputation, and even their wealth just to follow a star in the sky that they believed would lead them to the Jewish king.

This Christmas season, will you surrender your heart to Jesus? Will you lay down your daily agenda, your will, your hurt, your fear, and your dreams just to spend time with Him? Will you pray the prayer that Jesus told us to pray, "Your kingdom come, Your will be done, on earth as it is in Heaven"[13]? When we surrender our lives to Him, He returns to us all that He is—which is all that we need. In each one of these stories, the people surrendered to Him and in turn He gave them a purposeful and meaningful life. Today, offer yourself to Him and allow Him to transform your life into something so beautiful that it amazes you and impacts the world around you.

✹ ✹ ✹

Father,

I choose to surrender my heart, my life, my time, and my resources to You for your glory. May I not live for myself or want my own way. May each morning I humble myself before You and receive your heart for me, my family, and world around me. May I walk humbly before you and use all I am and have to know You more and make You known to this world.

Amen

DECEMBER 23

Go In *to* All *the* World

---

*Through the tender mercy of our God,
with which the Dayspring from on high has visited us;
to give light to those who sit in darkness and the shadow of death,
to guide our feet into the way of peace."*
—LUKE 1:78-79

*Go therefore and make disciples of all the nations,
baptizing them in the name of the Father and of the Son
and of the Holy Spirit, teaching them to observe all things that
I have commanded you; and lo, I am with you always,
even to the end of the age. Amen.*
—MATTHEW 28:19-20

*And you shall love the Lord your God with all your heart,
with all your soul, with all your mind, and with all your
strength. This is the first commandment. And the second, like it,
is this: "You shall love your neighbor as yourself."
There is no other commandment greater than these.*
—MARK 12:30-31

Our minds can have a psychological phenomenon called Inattentional Blindness. This occurs when our attention is focused on something else, making us unaware of what is right in front of us. I am sure you have experienced this phenomenon when you go to the refrigerator and can't find something, until someone walks up and shows you it is right in front of your eyes. Or when you're in a hurry to leave for work and you can't find your phone—that is laying on the table right in front of you or may even be in your hand.

Towards the end of the Christmas story, King Herod had the king of the world right in his territory town but was so blinded by his fear of losing his title, his authority, and his power that he missed his opportunity to meet the Savior of the world. Sometimes at Christmas we get so busy with the things we need to do and presents we need to buy, that we rush right past a hurting world who needs someone to see them. We can even get possessive of our time, our resources, and our love. We're willing to give a little, but please don't ask us to go out of our way because we already have too much on our plates. The reality is that we hold in our hearts the most priceless gift of a Savior who loves us and never leaves us. We hold in our hearts freedom from sin, His perfect love, and a hope of eternal life. We hold in us the God who heals, forgives, provides, and sets us free. How could we not share this amazing God with the world around us each day?

In Mark 16:15, Jesus told His followers to go into all the world and tell the wonderful news of what God has done for them through Jesus. I encourage you this Christmas to slow down and look into the eyes of those around you as if you are looking for God Himself. Many people in our world, in our cities, in our neighborhoods, and even in our own families may not know about the God of Christmas and His immense love for them unless we take the time to share it. Ask God to show you creative ways to love people and reach them with hope. Sometimes it is as easy as taking some cookies to a neighbor or giving a note of encouragement to a new person you meet at the coffee shop. Remember that God's amazing love reached out and saved you so you and I should freely give the same love to the world and the message of freedom He brings. Oh how He loves us!

✸ ✸ ✸

Father,

Thank You that You have given me Your amazing gift of love, salvation, and hope. I don't know where I would be today if I did not have You and Your love to wake up to each morning. I pray that I am generous with my time, my words, and my love to others. I pray You would lead me to people you want to me to love on and give me Your words to say to them. In a world that does not offer hope and pure love, may I be the light of Jesus.

In Jesus name, Amen!

DECEMBER 24

Light In *the* Darkness

For my eyes have seen Your salvation which you have prepared in the sight of all nations: a light for revelation to the Gentiles, and the glory of your people Israel.
—LUKE 2:30

Then Jesus spoke to them again, saying, "I am the light of the world. He who follows Me shall not walk in darkness, but have the light of life."
—JOHN 8:12

For with You is the fountain of life; in Your light we see light.
—PSALM 36:9

Let your light so shine before men, that they may see your good works and glorify your Father in heaven.
—MATTHEW 5:16

Jewish people celebrate a festival this time of year called Hannukkah which is also called the Festival of Lights. The festival is to celebrate how God rescued Jerusalem from their enemies and the two amazing miracles that happened during this time.

The first miracle was victory over the Syrians. The Maccabees, a group of Jewish rebels, revolted against their captors, and saved their land, their people, and their temple—the place where they worshiped God. The second miracle was that when they restored the temple, that the Menorah, a large candelabra, kept burning for eight days using only one small jar of oil to fuel it. This light kept the hearts and spirits of the Jewish people alive with hope.

This festival celebrates the rededication of the temple and the miraculous burning of the Menorah. The times of Hanukkah were similar to times when Jesus was born. The Jewish people were controlled by cruel King Herod. Like the Syrians, he tried to take away their rights to serve God and take away their freedom.

We also live in times where leaders have their own agendas, people can be cruel, and belief in the Bible is often criticized. But just as God granted victory to the Maccabees over the Syrian army and gave them the miracle of light, He also sent Jesus as a child-king in the midst of King Herod's evil rule, bringing light into their dark times. Still to this day, He is bringing His light into the dark areas of our world and of our lives so that hope may rise again. In John 8:12, Jesus says that He is the light of the world and if we embrace Him, we will not walk in darkness.

When light is given, shadows disappear and a clear path is illuminated. This Christmas season, ask Jesus to shine His light into your home, into your heart, and into your situations. His light brings hope, love, truth, and direction. His light removes the darkness, the doubts in our minds, and the shadows the enemy tries to use to scare us. His light helps us see things with the eyes of faith and victory. Just as God used one small Maccabean army to defeat the strong Syrian army and kept His light burning in the temple, so God is able to use the Light of Jesus to defeat the giants of our minds, of our lives, and of this world. Allow His light to shine into your heart today and illuminate it with faith! Then go be a light to someone else who's burdened by shadows of darkness this Christmas season.

❋ ❋ ❋

Father God,

Thank You for sending Jesus to be light and life to me and this world. I ask that you shine your light within me and conquer the areas in which the enemy tries to keep me bound. Allow Your light to shine so great in me, that it shines to others so they may see You in me.

In Jesus name! Amen

DECEMBER 25

The Most Beautiful Story

The next day John saw Jesus coming toward him, and said, "Behold! The Lamb of God who takes away the sin of the world!
—JOHN 1:29

And this will be the sign to you: You will find a Babe wrapped in swaddling cloths, lying in a manger."
—LUKE 2:12

Now to Him who is able to do exceedingly abundantly above all that we ask or think, according to the power that works in us.
—EPHESIANS 3:20

Merry Christmas! What a beautiful journey we have taken through the Christmas story. There is so much meaning and life inside this story. Today is such a special and beautiful day. It is not just special because of the lights, the trees, or the presents, it is special because God designed to demonstrate His amazing power, —leaping heaven to earth. He used ordinary people to reveal His glory and power so you and I may know Him. I pray over you today that you find your beautiful savior Jesus in every aspect of today and allow these moments to captivate your heart.

There is a scripture in the Christmas story that I pondered for a long time. In Luke 2:12, we see the story of the shepherds out in the field and the angel appearing to them in the sky. The angel told them to not be afraid for he had the most joyous news for the whole world—that the Messiah has been born today in Bethlehem. Then the angel said, "This will be the miracle or the sign of how you recognize that He is the Messiah, you will find Him wrapped in linen clothes and lying in a manger." The shepherds cared for Passover lambs by wrapping them in cloth and placing them in a manger filled with hay right after they were born, ensuring that they wouldn't be able to injure themselves, These lambs needed to be perfect, without blemish, so they could be offered as a perfect sacrifice for the sins of the people. This is the same way the shepherds found Jesus. Even though Jesus is the son of God, He came as a perfect sacrifice for our sins. That is why the shepherds recognized Jesus as the perfect Savior. When they found Him wrapped in cloth and lying in a manger, they knew He was a sacrifical "lamb" God was providing them. He revealed Himself to each person in a way that made sense and they understood.

Jesus is here today to reveal Himself to you in a way that speaks just to you. He is your healer, comforter, companion, and friend. Jesus was wrapped in cloth at birth, wrapped in cloth at His death on the cross, and He folded and left the burial cloth He was wrapped in the grave with when He arose again to life and victory! This Christmas season, may you see that God wants to do in your life all that He did in the story of Christmas. He wants to do miracles, fill you with vision, meet you with His presence, and fill you with the power of His Holy Spirit. God wants to move in your life, in your home, and in your town. Merry Christmas dear friend. May this day and all the days after this be filled with His hope, His amazing power, His presence, and His victory for of life! I pray you continue to seek Him as your treasure!

✻ ✻ ✻

Father God,

Thank You for the perfect gift of Jesus and how that You meet me right where I am at. Speak to me today in a way that I can understand. Help me to see You. May the wonder and awe of Your great love fill me and may I see all the beauty of Christmas today. Fill my heart with You. May I take this same beauty out to Your world so that they may know that there is a perfect Savior who knows and loves them.

In Jesus name!

ENDNOTES

1. Elvis Presley, Elvis' Chrismas Album. (RCA Victor 1957)

2. Isaac Watts, The Psalms of David: Imitated in the Language of the New Testament, and applied to the Christian State and Worship. (1719)

3. John Mayer, "Waiting on the World to Change," Continuum, (Aware/Columbia/Sony, 2006) Track 1

4. Isaac Watts, The Psalms of David: Imitated in the Language of the New Testament, and applied to the Christian State and Worship. (1719)

5. Mesfin Fekadu, The Associated Press. (2015) https://apnews.com/music-general-news-046b043a807b4d6ca57b4ae711817a86

6. C.S. Lewis, Letters to Malcolm: Chiefly on Prayer (San Diego: Harvest, 1964), 92-93.

7. James 1:2-4

8. Commonly attributed to Winston Churchhill, but neither the quotation nor parts of it can be found. https://richardlangworth.com/quotes-churchill-never-said-3

9. Isaiah 7:14

10. Micah 5:2

11. Micah 5:2

12. Numbers 24:17

13. Matthew 6:9-13

Made in the USA
Columbia, SC
17 November 2024

c43b1e5a-70a9-4a99-9733-cd88e4f48528R01